Little Sticker Dolly Dressing

Pets

Written by Fiona Watt

Illustrated by Lizzie Mackay

Designed by Johanna Furst

Contents

Best friends

Amber and Izzy love animals. Whenever they play with their toy animals, they talk about which pet they would choose. Amber would love to have a puppy, while Izzy would like any pet to look after.

Dress the dolls in their outfits, then decorate the pages with the rest of the stickers.

Izzy

Amber

Bonnie

Happy bunnies

Bonnie's been learning about how to look after
rabbits. She knows that they like to live in pairs,
what food to give them and that they need lots
of room to hop, stretch and play.

Sara

Lola

Playful kittens

Lola and Cassie don't have any pets of their own, but they've come to a cat café where there are lots of kittens to play with.

Cassie

Kirsty

8

Maddie

Collecting eggs

Twice a day, Kirsty checks the hen house to see whether
her hens have laid any eggs. She also makes sure
that they have lots of food to eat and water to drink.

Nadia

Winter walk

Nadia and Jessie have wrapped up in warm
clothes to take their puppies for a walk
in the snow. The puppies are great friends
and love to play together.

Jessie

Lara

12

Cleaning out

Every two weeks, Lara cleans out her gerbils' cage. She brushes out all the old bedding and replaces it with fresh shredded paper. She also washes all the tubes that the gerbils love to scamper along.

Billie

Lexie

At the stables

Every day after school, Lexie goes to see Peanut, her pony. She brushes his coat with a soft brush to get rid of any dirt or dust. She often meets Alesha who's looking after her pony, too.

Alesha

Anya

Robyn

Garden birds

Anya and Robyn don't have any pets, but they love
looking after the wildlife that visits their garden.
They fill the birdfeeder with things to eat and make
sure that there's plenty of water for the birds to drink.

Alina

Duck pond

Alina's family have a pond in their garden
where they keep lots of pet ducks.
She's invited Tamsin to come and help her
feed them, and to see the new ducklings.

Tamsin

Izzy

Feeding time

Izzy lives on a farm. It's really busy when the new lambs are born. Kara has come to help out and look after the lambs that need to be fed from bottles. She knows not to cuddle the lambs as she feeds them.

Kara

Lazy lizard

Tisha has a pet lizard called Ziggy, that lives
in a big glass tank. Ellie is fascinated to learn that
Ziggy eats insects and vegetables, and also loves
to lie for ages below a warm lamp.

Tisha

Ellie

A new puppy

Amber's dream has come true. She was so excited when she was given a puppy for her birthday. She's named him Baxter and is learning how to look after him. She knows it's important not to wake him while he's asleep.

Amber

Amber's top
and shoes

Izzy's top and
skirt

Happy bunnies
Pages 4-5

Bonnie's headscarf
and dress

Sara's outfit

Lola's top
and skirt

Cassie's
outfit

Cassie's
shoes

Collecting eggs
Pages 8–9

Kirsty's top and jacket

Maddie's sweater

Kirsty's skirt

Maddie's jacket

Maddie's skirt

Winter walk
Pages 10-11

Nadia's jacket

Jessie's hat and coat

Cleaning out
Pages 12-13

Billie's top

Lara's outfit

Lexie's top

Alesha's outfit

Lexie's boots

Garden birds
Pages 16-17

Anya's outfit

Anya's shoes

Robyn's top

Robyn's shoes

Duck pond
Pages 18-19

Alina's clothes

Tamsin's outfit

Feeding time
Pages 20-21

Izzy's outfit

Put Kara's top on first.

Lazy lizard
Pages 22-23

Ellie's clothes

Tisha's clothes

A new puppy
Page 24